EX LIBRIS

UNIVERSITATIS SANCTI JOANNIS

My Sister's Wedding

RICHARD ROSENBLUM

WILLIAM MORROW AND COMPANY   NEW YORK

Copyright © 1987 by Richard Rosenblum
All rights reserved.
No part of this book may be reproduced
or utilized in any form or by any means,
electronic or mechanical,
including photocopying, recording or by any information
storage and retrieval system,
without permission in writing from the Publisher.
Inquiries should be addressed to William Morrow and Company, Inc.,
105 Madison Avenue,
New York, NY 10016.
Printed in the United States of America.
1 2 3 4 5 6 7 8 9 10

Library of Congress Cataloging-in-Publication Data
Rosenblum, Richard.
My sister's wedding.
Summary: The author describes his sister's wedding,
including the preparations, the ceremony in the
synagogue, the actions of the rabbi, and the celebration
afterward.
1. Marriage customs and rites, Jewish—Juvenile
literature. 2. Weddings—Juvenile literature.
[1. Weddings. 2. Jews—Social life and customs]
I. Title.
BM713.R58 1987 296.4'44 86-16330
ISBN 0-688-05955-4
ISBN 0-688-05956-2 (lib. bdg.)

To Pam

One morning at breakfast my sister Sally told us she was going to get married to Larry. I was overjoyed. Now I would get my sister's room.

It was 1943, and Larry was in the U.S. Army Air Force, training to be a gunner. Sally was planning to go with him wherever he was stationed next.

I liked Larry. He was one of the older boys on the block who had enlisted when the war started. I missed listening to them talk about baseball and things.

My parents and Larry's parents had to make plans for the wedding. They had to see the rabbi, arrange for the synagogue and hall, hire a caterer for the wedding reception and a band for the music. They made long lists of wedding guests. It was a good thing we lived on the same block and had a lot of the same friends.

My sister and mother and grandmother went shopping all the time.
Besides a wedding gown, they were buying a whole lot of new clothes
for my sister. That's called a trousseau. In the evenings, they would
show the new things to my pop and me. Pop called it a fashion show.

Larry arrived the day before the wedding. He was a sergeant and wore gunner's wings over his breast pocket. Everett was Larry's best man. The best man is the groom's official helper at the wedding. He was a corporal in the army. Larry asked four of his friends to be ushers. Those are the guys who are part of the wedding and are escorts for the bridesmaids.

"Red" was in the navy, Newtie was a marine, and Benny was in the army. Shelly was already overseas, so I took his place as an usher. Shelly's girl Betty, who was a bridesmaid, wasn't very happy about having a kid as her escort.

The wedding was on a Sunday night at our synagogue. Doris, the maid of honor, came to our house early. Because my sister seemed nervous, Doris stayed all day and helped her get dressed and fix her hair. The doorbell rang constantly. Relatives came and went. I was in the middle of everything, opening the door, answering the phone, running errands, and feeling very important.

My father put on the suit he had rented. He called it his monkey
suit. My mother had an orchid corsage.

My father took me to the rabbi's office. Larry, Red, and Newtie were waiting for us. Larry signed the Ketubah, the Hebrew marriage contract. It told what the bride and groom had to do for each other. Red and Newtie signed it as witnesses.

My mother and sister were in a special room where the bride waited for the ceremony to begin. Her friends came to see her there. Larry wasn't allowed to see my sister until the wedding ceremony.

Downstairs in the party hall, I stood with Larry and the other guys, eating little frankfurters on toothpicks and knishes that the waiters brought around. The guys treated me just like I was one of them, and it made me feel very proud and grown up. Soon the room was very crowded with relatives and friends, and everybody was saying hello and shaking hands and hugging and kissing. Then it was time for the wedding to begin upstairs in the synagogue.

First the rabbi in his robes went down the aisle, singing a prayer. He stood under the wedding canopy. Then it was time for the ushers, each escorting a bridesmaid, to march in and stand on the side of the aisle.

The music started. The song was "Here Comes the Bride." Larry's sister Bunny, who was the flower girl, came down the aisle. Then my sister appeared, with my parents on each side of her. When she passed me, she winked.

The rabbi sang a blessing and performed the marriage ceremony
that made my sister and Larry husband and wife. The rabbi read the
Ketubah to the whole congregation. Larry and Sally drank wine from
a goblet, and then Larry smashed a glass that was wrapped in a napkin
with his foot.

That ended the ceremony. My father told me that the glass is
crushed so that we Jews should never forget the destruction of the
temple in Jerusalem thousands of years ago.

Doris helped my sister raise her veil, and she and Larry kissed.
Everyone yelled, "Mazel tov," which means good luck.

Downstairs in the big hall tables had been moved into the room. The bandleader, who was also the master of ceremonies, told everyone to be quiet. My sister and Larry were going to dance the first dance together. Then everyone got up and danced. Even me. I danced with Betty and my mother.

After dancing, we all sat down to the wedding dinner of roast chicken. Uncle Al came up on the stage. He read telegrams from President Roosevelt and Winston Churchill. I didn't realize he was fooling around until he read one from the king and queen of England.

The band started swinging and then the dancing really began. The guys and girls came out on the floor and started jitterbugging. That's a real fast dance that was popular then. One couple was so good that a little circle of people stood around them clapping and cheering.

The band played a kozatska, a Russian folk dance that men do.
They fold their arms in front and kneel down and kick to the music.

Then the band played a hora. We formed a big circle and a circle inside a circle. The circles moved faster and faster and people yelled and cheered.

The best dance of all was the conga. We formed a long line like a big snake, hands on the hips of the person in front, and one, two, three, kicked our way all around the room.

We went back to our tables because the lights were being turned
down. In the dark, a wedding cake was rolled out, and a spotlight
shone on it.

My sister threw her wedding bouquet at the bridesmaids. The one that caught it was supposed to be the next to get married. Betty caught the bouquet. I thought to myself, Shelly better get back for that wedding. I'm not going to take his place next time.

My sister and Larry were borrowing my Uncle
Jack's car for their honeymoon. When Larry
returned to where he was stationed, he found out
that he was going overseas immediately. That meant
that Sally couldn't join him. I never got her room
until Larry came home after the war.